Family

by

Joyce G. Knibb

Note for Librarians: A cataloguing record for this book is available from Library and Archives Canada at www.collectionscanada.ca/amicus/index-e.html

ISBN 1-4120-7800-8

Trafford's print shop runs on "green energy" from solar, wind and other environmentally-friendly power sources.

TRAFFORD
PUBLISHING

Offices in Canada, USA, Ireland and UK

This book was published *on-demand* in cooperation with Trafford Publishing. On-demand publishing is a unique process and service of making a book available for retail sale to the public taking advantage of on-demand manufacturing and Internet marketing. On-demand publishing includes promotions, retail sales, manufacturing, order fulfilment, accounting and collecting royalties on behalf of the author.

Book sales for North America and international:

Trafford Publishing, 6E–2333 Government St.,

Victoria, BC V8T 4P4 CANADA

phone 250 383 6864 (toll-free 1 888 232 4444)

fax 250 383 6804; email to orders@trafford.com

Book sales in Europe:

Trafford Publishing (UK) Limited, 9 Park End Street, 2nd Floor

Oxford, UK OX1 1HH UNITED KINGDOM

phone 44 (0)1865 722 113 (local rate 0845 230 9601)

facsimile 44 (0)1865 722 868; info.uk@trafford.com

Order online at:

trafford.com/05-2697

10 9 8 7 6 5 4 3 2

In Loving Memory of my Stoic Grandmother

née Annie May Gory

Gratitude

My gratitude is boundless for the gallant and enduring four who, once a month for nearly two years, came to my home and scoured every line and nearly every word and concept found in the manuscript. If there are errors, they can be attributed to my stubbornness and the manipulating of words to my liking. It would be unforgivable not to mention my husband as one who was also gallant and enduring throughout my creative throes.

These five are:

Elizabeth Allen

Victoria Bocash

Betty Challgren

Ethel Halsey

Russell Knibb

Note from the Author

If you have read *Let Us Speak of Pleasant Things and of Warm Places in the Heart,* you will once again meet a few of the people mentioned there in this new publication entitled *Family.* I have chosen not to entitle this new publication as *A Family, The Family* or *This Family.* I would like to think that the generic *Family* contains enough universality that it will strike a chord with many—no matter from what generation. This is not a memoir per se. Rather, it is an attempt to capture the complex relationships within the human family structure: the sharing, the loyalty, the strength, the caring, the ebb and flow of love, the laughter and the tears along with the joys and the sorrows found in most families. Of course, it is my family of whom I write.

Over the years, I have seen the structure of family change dramatically due to a myriad of reasons. It is indeed my personal feeling that every individual human needs a family to be there through thick and through thin. All too many of us function through a myopic sense that individually we are a total self...the core of the universe. How many times have I heard young people say, "No child of mine is going to change my life style." In that statement there is ignorance; there is selfishness, and there is an unbelievable callousness that freezes my heart. My response to that statement is: "Do the world—and yourself—a favor and do not start a family. There are enough lonely and lost children already in this world without your contribution."

There is no perfect family in this world; however, a family is certainly a sanctuary and a bulwark against the blows of life that will come. As one gets older, it is easier to see just what your family meant to you; how it shaped your character and determined most of your life...and usually for the better.

This writer, for one, is more than happy to have been born into a family unit that "held-to" old-fashioned concepts. However, it took me many years to realize the manner in which each member of the family had affected my life and those of my children. It is with gratitude that I recall the richness of the love, the understanding, the loyalty and the patience that were willingly given to me throughout the years. Sacrifices were made, but I do not think they thought of them as such. Rather, it was what parents, grandparents, uncles and aunts. did. All of my family's loving care humbles me beyond words. Please allow me to introduce you to a few of them whom I can never repay.

Contents

Annie May

Annie May was one of the three Gory Girls; all born on a sizable farm in Massachusetts not too far from the Rhode Island border. Her father was of Scots descent; her mother was from old New England stock with such family names as Williams, Aldrich, Arnold, Taft and Buxton. Grandmother's first name denotes a kind of girlish frivolity (almost a Southern sounding name). Her two sisters, Evelyn and Cora, were more suitably named. All three of them were tall and imposing women, though Annie May had a more slender frame. Evelyn and Cora would have been known as handsome women.

Studying an old sepia-toned photograph of my grandmother in her late teens or early twenties (dressed in a Gibson Girl blouse and a long black skirt while posed in profile), I would describe her as being somewhat exotic looking with black hair piled atop her head, dark almond shaped eyes and very high cheek bones...and more slender than I ever saw her. Of the Gory girls, Annie May was the only one who betrayed the Indian blood in her veins. This was not mentioned in polite society, and I have never been able to identify from which branch of the family this came to be. My father, and indeed, all of her children were not shy about the subject matter and tended to brag about their native American roots...as did the younger generation. The intermarrying between natives and English was not unusual in old families, especially those who settled in the hinterlands where women were scarce. Perhaps, it was made easier for some, as a company known as the "Boston Men" had sent missionaries into this area, and they had introduced the tall and friendly Nipmucs to Christianity. My grandmother could recall some of the Indians still living in the area when she was young...though she never spoke of them as having been of any relationship to her! In my childhood, it was not a popular concept. Annie May was a great source of historical information of the era past; she spoke of local lore and family history which she knew by heart. (On the other hand, her daughter, my aunt, was more interested in passing—to me—a broader perspective of national history.)

I have mentioned that I did not think her name suited her at all, and sometimes wondered where the Annie May of her youth went…or was it buried inside the tall and stoic grandmother that I knew? We lived only three houses from my grandparents, and I scooted back and forth over a worn path as soon as I was able to toddle and up through my late teens…when the tide began to change.

She was never the chubby, smiling face and hugging nature that grandmothers are supposed to have been. Quite the contrary, I cannot recall that she ever laughed or ever cried in my presence. She was solemn most of the time and never hugged or kissed me that I can remember. Yet, somehow, I knew she was always happy to see me at the door and always had something for me to eat, or more importantly, to do. (Young children have better antennae for this…they [the antennae] often disappear with age.) Looking back on the situation, I can only repeat what I heard as a youngster; she had married badly, suffered and endured for her four sons and one daughter. Both of her sisters would have gladly taken her in…but she had taken a vow for better or for worse…vows were honored in those days…and who is to say that this was not right.

I did not know it at the time, but I was highly valued in the family just for being a girl! For six generations my grandfather's family were granted only one girl in each generation no matter how many children were born…my great aunt Ella was his only sister, my aunt being the only girl in her generation followed by me in mine and my daughter in hers. Grandmother loved her four sons, but her daughter was her greatest solace and comfort from

Annie May Gory

the day she was born. I was the miniature daughter to Annie May. I knew she was never happier than when we were hunting for her precious mayflowers or for the sugar blues in the abandoned pastures. She had a blue enamel pail perforated with holes to keep the blueberries fresh and free of bruises. She had a little pail for me…which I still have. Her face became less stern and her frowns were gone as we sallied forth into the woods and the fields. I could not see it then, but I am sure the youthful Annie May was peeping through while her faithful shadow trotted behind her tall frame. She taught me all she knew about wildflowers, herbs and plants in general, though she did not care for gardening at home; she cared only for natural gardens found in the wild.

In the spring, Grandmother's small dining room and its large, walnut, gate-legged table of many leaves served a different and an important function. Extension cords were everywhere connected to lighted, goose-neck lamps around the edge of the table, sur- rounding boxes in which fertilized eggs were being incubated… Annie May's way. (Family members ate elsewhere while this was going on—much to their disdain.) When I was around five or so, I was allowed to be a part of the process.

Each morning, I would rush up to check on the eggs and was disappointed not to see the chicks hatching as promised. Boldly, I told her that she should add more lamps. Her reply was that nature takes its own time…and I should learn some patience. Finally, I was rewarded one day as we watched an egg begin to crack and could hear the pecking going on inside. Instead of a fluffy yellow creature, out came a very wet and soggy looking chick. I thought it rather disgusting in appearance. Nevertheless, I was fearful that it would not live. Grandmother made an excep- tion for this one and wiped him/her gently with a flannel cloth.

Others began to stir within the eggs but did not break through much to my dismay. She said to wait for a few minutes…if the egg was quite fractured and no pecking heard, we carefully took the egg apart and freed the chick…almost all of them lived. (I had already been warned that a few of them would not survive.) Soon others were hatching out all over the place. I stayed there the better part of the day until a few of them looked as expected. As she had said, "Nature has its own time schedule." Later, a miniature chicken-wire fence encircled the table in order to restrain a dozen or so yellow balls running about. The new generation stayed there until Grandmother felt they were ready for the coop and to move into the "real world." It was messy and a bit foul smelling in her house during this period. It was also curious that about this time, I had been informed that I was going to have a baby brother or a baby sister in August. I am not sure how many years it took me to connect these two events, but I am certain that I did not at the age of five…more likely I was trying to figure out how a baby could peck its way out of the egg.

Move forward a few years after Brother had arrived, and I had been given another chore to do for Annie May, who was still raising chickens for eggs to sell and as food for the table. After school, I would rush up to Grandma's house to help feed and/or water the hens and one miserable rooster. She had to go with me as the male of the species did not care for children…especially for this one. He would run at me squawking, trying to peck at my legs. Grandmother carried a broom with her and would swish his bottom with it. He finally got the idea. Although I had to carry the broom along with the pail of feed or water for as long as he lived.

Grandmother taught me a great deal about nature and life. At times, I felt the lessons were too harsh, but I have seldom ever been able to prove her wrong, excepting once. It was during one of these feedings that I was presented with one of her *harsh* lessons. The old family doctor had died, and I was bemoaning the fact and asking, selfishly, "What are we going to do now for our medical care?" Grandmother was in a bitter mood and gave me a scalding look. She said, "Put that bucket down." Which I did. "Now," she said, "put your hand in it." Which I did, growing curi

Annie May's Sister, Cora

ous as to where this lesson was going. "Now take it out." My hand was soon dry. "Did you see any change in the water after removing your hand?" Looking at the water, I could see no difference. "The water is life as was your hand while it was in it. That is how much one is missed after the hand is gone." I could have argued that the hand had absorbed some life and took it away, but I was so stunned I could not reply. I have thought about that lesson many times during my life. She was correct in one sense, we soon find replacements for life's needs, and the casual acquaintances soon fade from memory. Life and the present demand our attention, and we move on. Time even erases the communal past from our memories until those who find it fascinating begin to dig into it and report upon it for those who might find it interesting – though we never seem to learn from it. On the other hand, Grandmother was wrong. Those who have been loved are never far from the water. The proof is in my memories. I can easily visualize my adventures with Annie May while I was a small child and can recall her deep concern that I be prepared for what life might have in store for me.

It was both telling and upsetting when people who knew my grandmother, only superficially, described her in social conversation. I remember a school teacher who once said to me that she was so sorry for her...she looked so downtrodden and defeated by life. All this said to a ten-year-old who had not seen her grandmother through the eyes of society! Of course, I was furious. However, when I am hurt, I cannot respond to thoughtlessness or meanness as the case may be. Still, the drop of poison (awareness of the *gift of God to see ourselves as others see us* as Bobbie Burns would say) was in the well, never to be pure water again. (Innocent love does not blind the eyes but rather opens them to see loved ones in their true light.) I began to study Annie May with the cold eyes of a stranger...not easy to do. Yes, her shoulders were stooped and she was heavy through the middle (so unlike the proud, lithe girl in the photograph). Her hair was not a pretty gray; she wore it severely pulled back and rolled into a bun secured by large, tortoise shell hair combs. She cared little for her appearance…there were far more important things in life…such as bringing up a family of five.

I can not imagine that make up ever touched her face…she was above all that. Grandmother wore cotton dresses as did most housewives in this time period. Over these she wore a good, starched apron covered by another lesser apron (unstarched) and finally a really abused apron pinned to the second apron. This latter served as a towel of sorts to wipe off tomatoes plucked from the garden or to clean hens' eggs before taking them into the house. She would rarely wear the nice clothes given to her by family members as Christmas gifts; we finally gave up and gave her practical things that she could use in her daily, unfussy life. I can only recall her dressed for one occasion…at my wedding in the small community church with the reception held in the basement—the social hall for most New England early houses of God. Her shoulders were held back and her chin held high. She looked quite dignified—even elegant—in a navy and white print dress, her hair less severely drawn…and wore new, navy, laced shoes. I knew she would wear these for another ten years. I also knew the effort that she was making for her only granddaughter and former tag-along. How I wish that I had told her so at the time. I also wish that the thoughtless teacher had been there to swallow her words.

As Grandmother grew older, her cheekbones became more pronounced, her lips thinner, her eyes sunk deeper and her color-ing grew darker…almost a bronze color whether due to an illness or to DNA structure, I do not know. Now, it amuses me that others saw her as downtrodden and beaten by life. They had not known my grandmother or the Annie May of her children. My father used to call her by that name just to tease her. She would hit him across the shoulders with whatever she had in her hands, while he went out laughing. It is true that she was naturally shy

Annie May's Two Eldest Sons and Peggy

and had withdrawn from society mainly due to the poor circumstances in which she found herself. Though she did visit relatives in the small village where she lived or traveled up to New Hampshire to spend a few weeks with one of her sons (also to hunt for promising blueberry sites). I know this because I was with her. It was a matriarchal family; she ruled her nest with a firm hand. I never saw one of her children question her authority or dismiss her advice on personal matters no matter how old they became.

They were a bit afraid of her. Still as a youngster, I had gauged the lay of the land in her domain.

One early evening, I had perturbed my father for one reason or another—we were too much alike—and was about to get a swat on the bottom. Fortunately for me, he had a sprained ankle from tennis and was not as fleet as his six-year-old. I made a beeline for Grandma's house over the path while he had to stick to the smoother road. She always locked her screen door with a hook that I could have pulled out easily. I tugged on the door and yelled. She let me in, locked the hook and put me behind her skirts and aprons just as my father's angry face appeared at her door. He had to explain the "whyfore" of his anger at me. "Is that all?" she asked in a disdainful voice. "You did far worse than that as a youngster with no punishment meted out." Calling him by his first name she said, "Go home and cool off…I will bring her home in an hour or so." There was no argument; he was still furious, I am sure, but he did as he was told. She was as good as her word and took me home and delivered me to my mother. I was sent to bed while Grandmother stayed and talked to her son about the weather, the condition of the gardens and the local news. Nothing was said about an errant child, who was listening at the bedroom door. The incident was meant to be forgotten except by me.

World War II tested Annie May's courage and authority to the limit. She saw three young sons go off to war as they were expected to do…and did so willingly. My father, her eldest son,

Annie May with her Two Youngest Sons and her Only Daughter

wanted to volunteer; he could not bear to see his younger brothers off to serve their country without him.

Grandfather had more or less relinquished his role as caretaker and provider for his family; my father assumed the mantle. Grandfather was always a shadow figure seldom seen. He built them a home and from then on expected them to take care of themselves. He never ate with the family rather eating before or after they did. (He bought his own groceries just meant for himself.) Grandfather was usually in his carpenter's shop—much larger than the house-with its potbelly stove going all winter long. He did make me a rowboat one year with square ends so that I could not tip it over easily; my brother inherited it from me when I left home. My elusive grandfather was addicted to Zane Grey's westerns; he spent a great deal of time reading them in his room, smoking his cob pipe. Once in awhile, he would be home alone when I arrived and would tell me historical tales about the families and other interesting tidbits never heard before. He could tell a good story when he was a mind to do so. I think he was sometimes—most of the time—overpowered by the strong and independent personalities of his wife and his children.

At any rate, my father was determined to go to war until Grandmother sat him down to explain the facts. He had a family for whom he was responsible. Besides his wife and two children, he also would be the only one left to look after her and my aunt (who needed no looking after!). Chagrined though he was, he stayed—well sort of—he served his country putting up needed radio towers around New England. We saw him on the weekends. At least he was stateside.

Grandmother had pinned a large map of the world right on the living room wall. It was a wonderful geography lesson for me. We tracked where my uncles were training, and where they were later sent.

Most of the "victory mail" was censored; we never knew quite where they were all the time. She and I would go to the Saturday-afternoon shows just to see the newsreel, hoping to spot one of her boys, or at least the division they were in, featured in the war report. (She also liked to see movies with Sonji Henie in them.) If we gleaned where Patton or Bradley were from the newsreel, we would put a pin in the place mentioned as soon as we got back, knowing one of her sons was there as well. She had complete faith that three went and three would come home. Her spoken thinking was that three uncles in the family went to the Civil War and three came home—history did repeat itself. Annie May had taken care of one of the aging Civil War veterans herself…not to mention her own mother and my grandfather's as well. It was also Grandmother who patiently healed her youngest son from the seen and unseen wounds of the war.

Annie May was an avid reader; she was in seventh heaven when the book-of-the-month clubs came into being. She had already read all the classics and whatever else was in the small local library—read them several times in fact. She scoured the newspapers and read *The Grit,* a country weekly of sorts. She was my mentor as well as my censor in the matter of reading for pleasure or adventure: Defoe's *Robinson Crusoe,* Dickens' many long novels with some strong stuff hidden within them (I will never forget the lines from a film version of *David Copperfield* when the son, looking at his mother in her casket, said something to the effect that: it was not enough to be pretty…not enough to be good…one needed to be strong in order to survive life); a few of Shakespeare's dramas, *Julius Caesar,* of course, *Romeo and Juliet,* along with Mark Twain's *Tom Sawyer* and *Huckleberry Finn* met with her approval. She would be amazed to know that some of these have been taken from children's book lists and considered dangerous to young minds today. We also read *Gulliver's Travels* by Swift, strictly as an adventure story…this edition had some deletions from the original. It wasn't 'til college that I realized the bitter satire for what it was. When Pearl Buck's *The Good Earth* arrived at the library, I was anxious to read it. Grandmother had to read the book first. She decided that this was a bit too earthy for me. She said, "It is too risky." Already a smarty in high school, I said that she meant risque.

She pursed her lips and said, "No, it is too risky." Reading it in later years, I realized that she had chosen the correct word…it was not "risque" but "risky" reading for a teen-age girl. I had foolishly corrected her grammar and pronunciation a few times—very few. She always said the word, *figure,* in the British way, though I did not know it at the time. "Grandmother, it is not fig-ah; it is fig-yure with a heavy accent on "g" and "yure." "Maybe for some," she sniffed. I learned in later years that many of the old New Englanders' mispronunciations were merely words that had not been colonized at the time. (Now, it is back in fashion for those educators who finally travel to Europe. Grandmother was ahead of her time.) As the years rolled on, she knew that she was losing her tag-along to the wider world and remained stoic as ever. That is not to say that I still did not dash up to see her—now having to take the road as buildings intervened—with some exciting news or to show her a new dress for school, etc. I still landed there for comfort and security, though sadly I never knew how much I had loved her by being her constant companion, or how much she had loved me by showing me the joys of nature and preparing me for the ups and downs life might have in store.

Thanksgiving was Annie May's command performance day. She minded not where we went for Christmas or any other holiday as long as all (including daughters-in-law…no son-in law ever to be as her daughter never married) were seated around the many-leaved table that filled the dining room with little space to spare. Only hospitalization or overseas duty kept the family members away. For youngsters it was an exciting time when cooking was raging in different kitchens. I had been assigned a task that I performed until I flew away. Walnuts had to be cracked to obtain the unbroken meat of the nut, dates were pitted and replaced with half of a fat marshmallow with the perfect half of a walnut…then the whole rolled into powdered sugar. The delicious treat was respectfully placed in an amber colored dish that I thought truly beautiful. At the time, I did not know it was carnival glass.

It is still treasured and rests proudly in the hutch of my dining room...with all the memories intact.

As the years rolled by, I began not to look forward to Thanksgiving Dinner around that long table where the jokes were always the same, the political arguments rehashed in the same old way...and finally the game of cards to come. Grandmother had one vice and that was playing cards...not for money rather for the fun of it. Everyone was expected to play a round of cards to see who would wash the dishes piled high in the sink. I did not like to play cards – still don't. But, I learned how to plays Hearts very well. Though at times, I still ended up with three others to clean up the aftermath – because "the boys" cheated. Still, I would give anything to return to the noisy crew assembled around the table, for a taste of great-aunt Evelyn's plum pudding steamed in a tin pail and accompanied by a delicious sauce, a rare treat that one could afford once a year. I would even put up with the teasing from the uncles and enjoy the wit and companionship of my aunts...even endure my pesky brother's tricks to get attention. This was the one day of the year that Annie May was in her glory with her family all around her with plenty of food and the usual banter of the clan when it gathered once a year. Even Grandfather could not resist coming in from his shop to join in the family celebration – though he still did not sit down and eat with us. No one seemed to mind...everything was the way it was. I do not believe my grandmother laughed even on Thanksgiving Day; she did not have to do so as she glowed with happiness and was content.

The dark walnut table – inherited from Grandmother's family – that filled the room was the setting for many good times that Grandmother's children shared with family and neighborhood friends. It is not difficult to realize that Annie May and her table were the center of much of their lives. I hear tell of card games served with popcorn and hot chocolate during the winter months when the table was filled to capacity with her growing family and those of the neighborhood. Grandmother was right in the midst of it…and playing to win. When serious discussions were to be had, we gathered at the table—sometimes many—other times few. Here we were near the radio when the president had an important announcement or some vital war news was to be heard. The table also had medical uses: When Grandmother became diabetic, I had to go up and give her insulin shots (which we both dreaded) while her daughter was at work. My aunt was the neighborhood RN and cleaned and bandaged many a youngster's wounds around the table. Here dress patterns were cut out as well as complicated pieces for a quilt. Letters were written and carefully read on the hard wood. It was a table that had seem many uses and much life. Its vitality could be felt even when it was just Grandmother and I sitting at it. (Years later, my aunt had it refinished and placed in her kitchen/dining room.)

There were no tears of protest from Annie May when I flew away to view the world. Not even any lectures on my behavior… those lessons had already been given over eighteen years of time. If I had not learned them by then, I never would. She had known I would go; they all did at one time or another. Perhaps, she also knew I would be back; she had that intuitive insight into people (and thereby trusted few of them). When I returned home with fractured wings, she said not a word and quietly returned to her old ways of helping me to grow. I was the only grandchild—or great-grandchild—whom she invested so much of herself into, expecting me to retain the knowledge and to make use of it. I hope I have not failed her in any way. Love need not be loud or even verbose to be heard and to be felt.

Brother

He came into my life when I was half a decade old – certain ages have more landmarks than others.

One would have thought that I would have been jealous after being the only grandchild – and a granddaughter at that – for all those years. I suspect my only thought, at the time, would have been of having another playmate in the neighborhood gang (this word did not bear the connotation of today), and that I would finally have a brother or a sister as did everyone else. In a gentler age, five-year olds were not burdened with the knowledge of the birth process as they are in our brave new world. When the time drew near, I was gathered up by good friends of the family and taken to their home twelve miles away. I was excited to go on this new adventure, never having been far from home without members of the family. My memories of these two weeks were the smell of cigar smoke in the husband's den and the shining of the wood on the stairs going to the bedrooms. Their house was as neat as could be; they had no children of their own; I was treated like a breakable toy.

Before I left on *vacation,* changes were being made for the newborn to be. The dining room furniture was moved elsewhere to be replaced by a bed, cradle, small table and a few chairs. Brother would be born in the same room that I had been. This room was close to the pantry and the kitchen; a small serving door opened into the dining room (which we later used as the balcony in our productions of *Romeo and Juliet*) where meals and other necessities could be easily reached. I cannot recall that I was worried about my mother…little was said to make me be so. One morning, I was told that I had a baby brother weighing in at twelve pounds with a good set of lungs. Naturally, I wanted to go home immediately, but I was told that I had to wait a few days as mother needed to rest…small wonder! Each day crawled by. I became more restless and rather cranky. It was Grandmother who finally said I should come home. The twelve miles home seemed endless. I dashed out of the car and through the back door and into the dining room. My fragile mother was still in bed with dark circles under her eyes, but she was smiling and holding something in a bundle of blankets. My first thought was that he was very small and would not be playing outside for sometime to come…which was a big letdown. Later, my mother allowed me to hold him or watch him while she did other things. In the crib, he would kick his feet and wave his hands as though grasping for something. Sister was thrilled when he would catch one of her fingers and hold on with a good grip to be accompanied by gurgles and smiles.

Brother was rather well developed when he was born. As the days crowded one into the other, he began to look as though, in time, he would be a worthy playmate. His eyes had already turned dark brown and were round, unlike my almond shaped ones. He had a healthy growth of thick, dark hair and long, dark lashes…of which, I admit, I have always been jealous. One could not have asked for a better natured baby; he was happy and content…and had my mother's sweet disposition. Although he did have a streak of mischievousness. Before one would think it, he was toddling around on his chubby legs and with merry eyes looking for something to get into. He got into his father's radio room and rearranged a few things; he got into his mother's vanity table and sprinkled powder and perfume around; the last straw was his getting into the shed and into some paint.

Rather than try to hold onto *quicksilver*, my father decided to fence it in. He built a play house for my brother; a sizable one at that with a shingled roof, wooden floors, small steps as the floor was raised in order that he could see *far and wee*. It was about the size of a large room or a small camp. The sides were covered

Sister and Brother

with large spaced chicken wire and a sturdy door secured him within. At first, Brother thought this was great and played to his heart's content...until he realized that the rest of the neighborhood gang were running free. He would cry little tears and then bigger ones and finally would howl. My mother was not happy with this, but Father said, "He will get tired of that howling soon." Which he did not. Next, he was taking off all his clothes; this would guarantee that my mother would come and put them back on. I was not happy with this project from the start; I did not want my brother in a chicken coop and foolishly told my father so. "Fine," he said, "You can watch and care for him during the day." I had bitten off more than I could chew. Five other youngsters and I were exhausted at the end of an afternoon, taking care of Brother. During the summer months, Grandmother came up with a solution: If he promised to play in his pen in the morning hours, we would all go up to camp – a mile up the road and not half as well built as the playpen – to swim and to cook out for lunch and maybe a supper as well. At some point, the playhouse was torn down, much to everyone's satisfaction. I did not know it, but it was a sign that Brother was too old for this and that there would be no more sisters or brothers in the family.

He became my tag-along as I had been to my grandmother. It was difficult for me to sneak away; either he would catch me trying or Mother would say, "Take your brother along, he wants to go too." As a consequence – though he would never admit it – it was I who taught him how to swim, skate and play baseball. He was afraid of the water; a fear I never had. I would row him around in our square ended boat to show him that there were no monsters in the deep water. Much to my satisfaction he became an excellent swimmer; as an adult he was in seventh heaven when he body surfed in some rather angry looking waves. I can still see him surfing through the water in Cancun, like a native, while my daughter watched in envy.

In the winter when the ponds were frozen over, I liked to

skate alone on an old ice pond—where they had once cut and stored the ice in sawdust in the still standing barn. In order to do so, I would dash home after the bell, change clothes, grab my skates and be off before Brother got home. He dawdled along the way studying this or that. If Mother would catch me, I would have to wait for my sibling, put his skates on etc. One day I managed to escape undetected, flew across the fields and sat down on the old dam to put on my skates. Much to my disgust, I saw signs of my brother's mischievousness. He had taken the shoestrings out and rethreaded them…from the top down! By the time, I had restrung the laces, Mother and he had arrived. None of us said anything at all…but my brother was grinning.

He was even tempered like his mother. Unlike his sister or his father—who thought it was great sport—, he never argued with anyone. He grew into a quiet and a gentle man. Still, if he had been hurt or was angry enough, he would find a quiet form of retaliation. He was in his young teens, when for some reason or other, he had been grounded. In his eyes, it was not fair. Mother had done the grounding this time. While she was out for the afternoon, he carefully placed thumb tacks on the felt of every hammer on my mother's aging upright piano. She enjoyed playing her religious hymns as well as Marie MacDonald's and Nelson Eddy's current and popular songs. She would only play the piano when no one was around, as we all teased her about Nelson Eddy. The house was quiet as she sat on the piano stool; she was amazed to hear her sweet songs sounding like ditties from a barroom piano.

Everyone thought it was clever, amusing and a harmless prank…except Mother, though she laughed, later. Thus, another family legend was born. Brother's only punishment was to take the tacks out as carefully as he had placed them in. He played piano and string instruments by ear. Much to my chagrin, as I could count no special talents of my own. He also knew I disliked the *Glow Worm* piece. If he saw me coming, he would rush to the instrument of my torture and begin to play and sing, *Glow little glow worm...glitter, glitter* and so on, trilling the keys for all they were worth.

Like most country and family loved children, he was shy out of his comfortable sphere or in a social setting...so was I but I hid it better...for the most part. The family was surprised when his graduation came along; he and a friend got up and sang and played their ukuleles á la Arthur Godfrey. Unfortunately, Sister was elsewhere at the time.

My only advantage – if it were an advantage – over Brother was that I, was the better athlete...quicker responses, ran with good speed and had decent hand and eye coordination...much to my father's dismay...why waste that talent on a girl was his thought. My only sibling had his heart set on playing hockey. In this community guys who played this sport were equivalent to Greek Olympians and were the beneficiaries of many rewards. The neighborhood gang played a pick-up hockey game on the ice pond. I, of course, was the forward man. Brother, who was not fleet of foot or quick of movement, being more deliberate and accurate, was goalie. (I am writing about this as I wish to dispel the myth that I broke my brother's nose whilst playing hockey... which is not true...I don't know when he broke his nose, but I was not on the scene at the time...here is the myth stripped to the truth.)

One Thanksgiving we had a few hours or so to skate before dinner. Brother wanted to practice his goalie skills. I was shooting the puck at the goal for him to push away or block. He kept saying, "Hit it harder, hit it harder, right here!" I was happy to oblige and sent it exactly where he was pointing. It hit him right in the mouth – we were not into face guards at the time – and chipped two of his front teeth. He had them filed down later in life. I never lived it down in family circles; like other myths it has grown and changed shape.

Like our mother (and unlike his father and sister) he had the

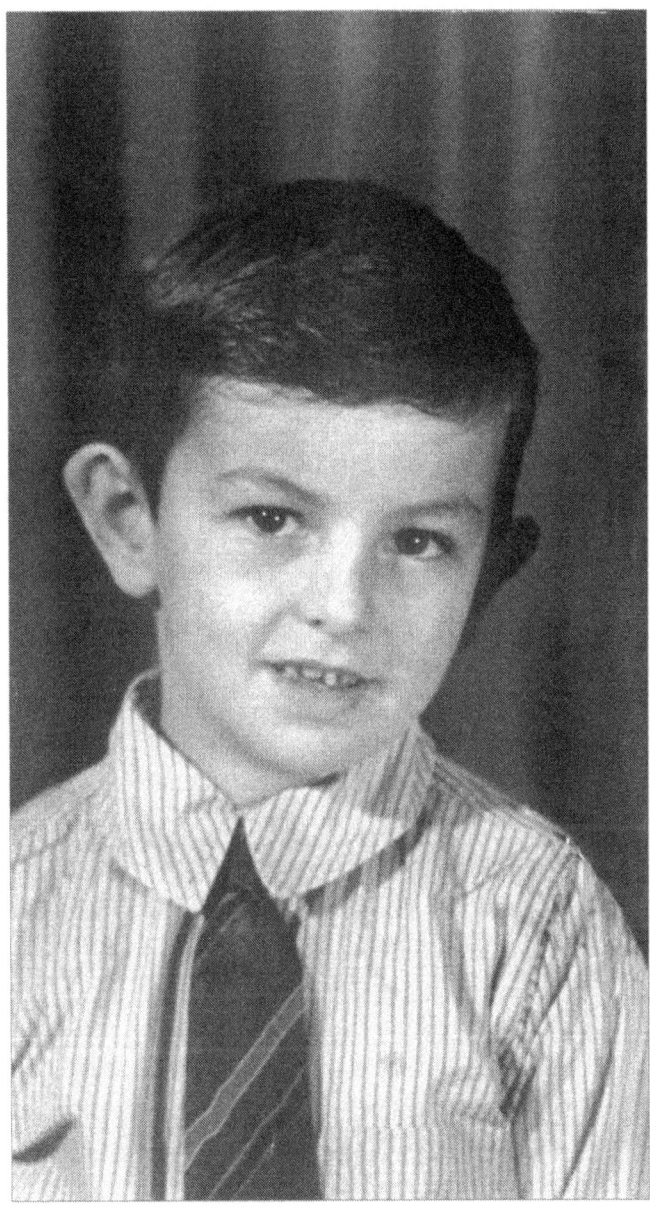

The Mischievousness Shines Through

patience of a monk. I can see him now building small, model air-planes with mere match sticks. How he did this with his chubby hands, I do not know. Every year the planes became larger and more complicated. Soon it was balsa wood and the fabric of the plane was coated with dope…a paint whose odor permeated the house for days. Airplanes were his passion…a passion that lasted throughout his life. The theme of his graduation from high school was aviation; the models of airplanes constructed by the class members were suspended from the auditorium ceiling…his were among them.

After a stint in the Air Force (what else?), he always man-aged to have a plane or co-owned one the remainder of his life. I can recall the first time that he took me up in his *fighter plane.* (Snoopy would have wished one like it to fight the Red Baron.) After I managed to boost myself up the side of the plane, it was necessary to shove back the clear top in order to climb into the tiny back seat, then reach over to pull the cover closed, sealing oneself into the plane. Now, I was no stranger to flying but not in this unpressurized, noisy and smelly antique. We had to yell to each other to be heard. It was hot inside the plane, no air condi-tioning here. I wanted to slide back the top to get some air, but he said no way. "You will fall our or something. I just know it!" He was a cautious pilot; nevertheless, even his little plane maneuvers turned his sister green. He was quite put out and said, "I will nev-er take you up in a plane again." And, he never did. Though, he talked his favorite aunt and uncle into taking a spin—in a much better plane, I might add. Aunt was dreadfully afraid of flying but had promised him that she would go up with him when he had his own plane…and she did…and made a much better show of it than I did.

One of the highlights of our father's life was an extended trip with his son to the American Southwest. They flew from spot to spot; my father quickly learned the many complications of flying, landing and storing one's plane. He had always been somewhat disappointed that my brother was not an enthusiastic sports' team participant...nor did he follow in his father's footsteps. After this flight, my father came back with a great deal of respect for his son, and their relationship became closer. Before his marriage, Brother and our parents vacationed together...they were given the time to enjoy each other as adults rather than the oft-times strained relationships between adult children and parents. (Parents have to give up the nurturing role...not easy to do. Adult children need to see their parents as human beings...neither saints nor sinners...in order to become good friends in the adult world.)

Though Brother did play ice hockey in high school—as a goalie—he did not find his niche in team sports. Rather, he fine tuned his own likes that were more individualistic and suited his natural talents: Such as flying, skiing, golfing, swimming, surfing, hiking, camping ,fishing or building anything from boats to airplanes for his own use. I cannot claim any influence upon the perfection of his skiing except for the fact that he started out on and used my skis for many a year...finally bringing them back to me for my children to use.

Not far from our childhood home was a steep hill in an abandoned pasture. Here, bundled up beyond recognition, we spent hours in the winter months sledding...with Sister often pulling Brother up the hill on the sled...as my father had done with his younger brothers and sister on the very same hill. We suffered bumps and bruises from this sport, colliding with other sleds, falling off them, getting tongues stuck on the metal part of the steering handles. I had warned Brother a million times not to do this...but every child has to try it at least once. (It is a scary sensation when one layer of skin is left behind if one tries to take it off too quickly.) At any rate, one winter I received a handsome set of skis. Sled was quickly relegated to my sibling while I practiced my short lived skiing career. We never knew enough to zigzag down the hill but went straight down the trail for all we were worth…I have the scars to prove it. As soon as I left home, Brother commandeered the skis and before too long was skiing down New England trails, then onto those in Colorado and in Switzerland. In the latter, he banged his knee badly; he never forgave the whole of Europe for this incident, refusing to return ever again. "Snow was not the same in Switzerland," he said, "There is a different consistency and composition." Though I never saw him ski, his style became legendary among those who knew him. He had taught himself how to ski and had a distinctive style. He did not crouch over as the professionals do, but stood more or less straight up with slightly bent knees and swished down the hills with ease and style. Brother also had a strict dress code that included a Swiss hat and an unlighted pipe. Many have told me that he was poetry in motion once he was on his skis and moving like the wind down the trails…or better still on no trail at all.

He was about thirteen years old when I ventured out into the world. At the time, he was slimming down from the chubby, little brother and growing tall at a wild rate. Thereafter, we went our separate ways and saw each other only on brief visits, weddings and funerals. Once when I was home, he flew back for his class reunion. He dug out his high school sports jacket, shirt and tie. Sister said, "you're not going to wear those are you?" He had put on some weight and height…late growth stage. "Why not?" he replied. The jacket was short in the sleeves and could not be buttoned; the tie was a fifties affair calling attention to any beholder. It all matched well but did not fit well. Nevertheless, he went sailing out with his old suit and tie saying that he wore this so that his former classmates would recognize him. I was sure of that! (He was the same little brother in disguise as an adult.) His good disposition remained with him from childhood through adulthood.

Quiet and soft spoken, he turned away from wrath as the Bible suggests. People naturally went to him for advice and comfort. Having no children of his own, he guided many a friend's

High School Jacket and Tie…When They Fit

youngster on the right path...this included teaching them to hike, camp and ski...following in the footsteps of his aunt who guided other youngsters in a different manner. (Perhaps those who choose not to marry or do not have children serve a greater purpose by being temporary parents to many other people's off-spring. Uncles and aunts – family related or not – are so necessary for young children; they are the second line of defense and often provide a link between parent and child when the troubled years arrive during the budding drive for independence and identity.) Brother and I had several aunts and uncles to smooth our way and to introduce us to new experiences: such as camping, ice fishing and the like as well as traveling and saturating us with history. Not to mention the much needed help now and then.

Though Brother became a responsible and a hard worker, he never outgrew his tendency to play practical jokes upon the un-wary. His wife was not immune from his long thought out quiet and mild revenges. In later years, she said she grew to like his oft-times teasing. He only did this to people that he liked or loved. It was necessary to learn how to read him as he was not an open book: Brother carried his wounds silently and stoically not shar-ing them with anyone...reminding me of Annie May. Still, he was not opposed to laughter and the enjoyment of life.

Along with his skiing style, his chuckle was as well known and remarked upon...I can clearly hear the sound of delight coming from him at a tender age...many were surprised to hear this from a baby. With age his chuckle grew in size until it engulfed him as well as those in his presence. It would start out somewhere in the pit of his stomach, roll up through his chest and on through the throat, leaving him shaking with laughter. It was contagious and listeners of his jokes would start to rumble with laughter them-selves before he ever reached the punch line. He was convinced that life was to be enjoyed (and thought his sister too serious and dour, I know). Despite a few setbacks, he was able to cram his life full of what he considered pleasurable. This included flying, swimming, surfing, hiking, camping, skiing, golfing, friendships and good dining. Hunting was not in his vocabulary; he was especially interested in animals of the wild…studying their ways for hours without moving. Pursuing some of these pleasures, he found his true home in the mountains of Colorado.

As you know, he was no stranger to mountains, taking over my position as companion to our father on his annual pilgrimage up Mt. Washington. Mountains became a part of his life: to climb up them, to camp in them and to ski down them. Somewhere along the line he outgrew New England; it became too confined for him both literally and figuratively (I hear a similar tale from my offspring!). He liked the fact that in the wild west people were more friendly and open as most of them came from elsewhere, thereby not being as grounded in tradition or as confined by definitive beliefs. In Colorado he discovered a place that not only spoke to him – as did New England to me – but also provided many of the ingredients that allowed him to pursue his fun things. The wide open spaces and the magnificent vistas suited him just fine, thank you.

Brother found a spot and built his own home…not completely satisfied with it, he found a more secluded spot to build his second home. "Bigger and Better" was his motto. He was thinking of creating a third home farther in the mountains. His wife wisely put her foot down and said this is the "Bigger and Better" one, right here. The carpenter genes shine through the male members of the family; there appears to be a compulsion to build. When I say he built his home…I mean just that: he built it himself with a bit of aid now and then from his father…only using professionals when all else failed. (His nephew [our son] also heard the call of Colorado, following in his uncle's footsteps even to the point of building his first log home in the mountains. Had he lived longer, my father would have had a home in the mountains as well…the site already purchased.) Brother as a child had always said, "I can do it myself." No one ever questioned that he could not "do it himself."

Both of us became busy with careers and in my case a family to raise as well; we became separated both in distance and in shared experiences. We did not know each other as adults. I do recall a wedding that we both attended when a lively blonde came up to him for the next dance. (A *risky number,* Annie May would have said.) Off he sailed to the dance floor…while I blurted out, "My brother cannot dance and certainly cannot do the rumba." A friend of his smiled and said, "There is a lot you do not know about your brother." How true it was, and it saddened me. We only shared one mini vacation together with his wife and our daughter in Cancun. The laughter and memories flowed from us as well as a few misadventures while sightseeing. At Chichen Itza, he insisted on climbing the long and steep temple stairs as he had left his camera behind on the first trip up. Bum knee and all he re-climbed the dizzying stone stairs in order to get a view from the top on film. I would not climb at all, after seeing the guards go up to bring people down who refused to come down. Descending was an eerie experience; few knew enough to zigzag–as in skiing steep slopes–down the steps in order not to feel as though one were walking off into space. Sitting on the fine sandy beaches of Cancun, we watched him body surf like a native to his heart's content. In the family room is a picture of the five of us sitting around a table in Casablanca-like surroundings with a piano in the background playing–as I recall–*As Time Goes By.* We looked so happy…time and distance were erased for a little while.

When everyone had finally retired, I had great plans to become reacquainted with my brother and more acquainted with my sister-in-law. We had managed to get out to Colorado for brief amounts of time. The last time we were there, a family reunion at Christmas time in California was in the making. (Husband and I along with an uncle and an aunt, who live in New Hampshire, are the last survivors of New England!). In June, I received a birthday card from him, which surprised me as his wife–like many others – usually sent the cards. The verse made me smile, knowing he thought I was over serious about life in general. It read, *Have a happy heart/today and always,* with his signature on it. It bothered me a bit: I did wonder about the change of routine. Five days later, I became irritable, ill tempered and restless. I just knew something was wrong…not the first time this scenario had occurred to me…usually with good reason. My husband said we best go somewhere to take my mind off whatever it was. While in the car, I said, "Something terrible has happened." Someone was trying to reach me; I was unable to make the connection. It was eleven-thirty in the evening when the phone rang; I was reading as I could not sleep. "Here it is," I said to myself. It was my sister-in-law crying so I could not understand her, but my heart stopped beating. "Your brother is gone," she said. I could not accept those words, foolishly thinking he had gone somewhere or other without her blessing. "No, he has gone from all of us." He had passed over, as I like to say, on his father's birthday and his memorial service was a few days later on the birthday of his namesake, our eldest son.

There had been a strange set of circumstances. He and his wife were vacationing in British Columbia. Brother wanted to go up to Whistle Mountain in the morning; his wife, having a miserable cold, stayed at the time share. When he had not returned by late afternoon, she called the police. Brother was found – having pulled his car off the road in order not to cause any problems. He had died alone with a violent heart seizure. If police and hospital records are accurate, he went about the time that I had said, "Something terrible has happened." It is true, I was furious that he had been alone, but upon further reflection, I knew this was his way. He had been where he wanted to be – in the mountains and alone.

Nature kindly numbs us with shock so that we can function somewhat. We flew out to Denver where our youngest son and his wife met us and drove to the church. It was sizable. It was also filled with his friends, former co-workers and those to whom he had been kind. His wife had asked certain friends to compose their own thoughts about the life of my brother. Many would compose, but few were able to give the eulogies themselves…it is not an easy task. One man bravely read them all.

The summary of these individual eulogies moved me beyond measure…as it did to many others. His young nephew sitting beside me wept without shame. We heard about Brother's love for the great out-of-doors, his distinctive style of skiing, his love of camping with friends and climbing mountains, his unique chuckle and his sense of humor, his love of life and congenial personality. One young man wrote that he was the only father he had ever known…Brother taking on the role of a father for a youngster who had not known his own. Co-workers spoke of his reliability, his fine-tuned knowledge of his craft, and his quiet authority along with his understanding and kindness. His wife's words gave the best description of my brother and what he had meant to her. The gentle giant was a huggable bear to all. Without thinking, I said," I wish my parents could be here; they would have been so proud." A stranger kindly put her arms around me and said, "They are here; they are here."

Youngsters wrote about his effort to have them feel the satisfaction of hard physical work while camping. Wood was chopped with an axe or cut with a handsaw…no newfangled tools…it was necessary to stay in tune with nature. I smiled when those who climbed with him would question, "How much farther?" Only to hear a familiar reply with just one word changed, "over the next ridge"….and the next one and the next one until everyone groaned when they heard the reply…just as I had done so many, many years ago. (Traditions *are* a permanent connection between generations.) I was amazed that my shy and gentle brother had befriended so many and had been loved and respected by so many others. It was a great comfort to me and also revived my faith–somewhat–in mankind. Whatever he did, Brother did his best, and his best was so much better than most. Upon reflection, I realized although we had spent too many years apart, he had remained the same lovable, chubby child that I had known for those short thirteen years. Memories of those years are a wonderful thing to have and to hold.

Back at Brother's home in the hills, an old friend of his took me downstairs to show me the experimental plane that Brother had been building for some time. Piece by piece, the larger match sticks were glued together. The design was on the wall, and he wanted an engine that would make it the fastest small airplane in the world. If he had ever finished it, he would have had to tear down one side of the basement to get it out...which he would have done, of course. We both concluded this project was a work in progress...perhaps never meant to be completed...something that was there to work endlessly upon in an attempt to reach perfection.

Brother was laid to rest with many other veterans around him. He has a wonderful vista of the mountains surrounding him. How I regret those years that we were apart and failed to share each other's life as we had done as youngsters. I can still see him now with those large brown eyes looking at me to take care of any situation that might arise while we were growing up. Then the tears come, some seen, some unseen. He left us all behind way too soon. My memories of our youth flood through my mind every so often, leaving me both sad and happy...the bitter sweetness of life gone by never to return. It was a good life full of innocence, sharing, loving, hard work, tears and laughter. It was a good time to have been brought up with family surrounding us and protecting us as well as letting us go. I am so proud of him and so pleased that he came into my life. Please, cradle his soul gently.

She might, at one time, have been a wiry five-two, always struggling to maintain the necessary ninety-eight pounds to satisfy health and life insurance policies. Work, illness and time have whittled her down to less than five feet, and she weighs in at a pathetic sixty-five. The struggle then, and now, to retain weight was due to her tremendous will and drive, burning up the caloric intake before it had a chance to solidify.

The physical nature mirrored the spiritual as her *output* was consistently greater than the intake received. A small bundle of energy directing itself at specific goals and specific aims to be accomplished not tomorrow or the next day—but today! She was born to move with a no-nonsense step up and down hospital corridors followed by the swish, swish of the starched white uniform; her head held high and topped by a starched cap with the hard won black stripe across its band.

Sitting by her bed watching her today while the white, white hair catches the sunlight and those eyes, now huge from the surrender of the flesh around them, pursuing something interesting...something to do. Is the cover straight enough? Are those tissues on the bed? Are the dressings clean and secure? Even though the frail and voiceless body cannot do or say, her eyes direct me to do what ought to be done.

She is my maiden aunt of seventy-three years, not really that old when we consider the spryness of many senior citizens today. But a lifetime of giving, caring and doing for others, intermingled with serious bouts of illness, have quite literally worn her out. She has been many things to many people: daughter, sister four times over, a friend and mentor to many, filling out each of these relationships to its fullest connotative and denotative meaning.

Above all, she was an RN giving one-hundred percent of her body and soul while she attended upon those who were in need of professional and competent nursing care. For thirty-nine years, her footsteps of purpose and confidence echoed through the hallways of a nearby hospital, first as a floor nurse and later as head nurse and instructor. I am sure that there are still many who will recall Miss Green, or "Greenie," as she was known to her peers, and feel a debt of gratitude for her bulldogged determination and unflagging diligence for placing the care and comfort of the patient above all else.

It was rare to go anywhere with her—and I was often at her heels, trying to keep up—without a former patient approaching us and telling me what a crackerjack nurse she was, and that she, in some special way, had rescued him or her not only from a serious disease but also from the soulless medical methods oft times encountered during the healing process. At an early age, I towered above her in height but somehow felt vastly smaller and awesomely insignificant in her presence...I still do.

Today's *catergorizers of* mankind—and womankind—would no doubt label Miss Green as a workaholic, an over-achiever, a perfectionist, inner-driven and further derogatory terms to describe characteristics, all of which were considered, in bygone days, virtues not vices. A capsule account of her securing the coveted title, RN, would decidedly illicit groans from more prosperous and pampered generations, who cannot believe that so many odds ever presented themselves or so much determination existed to overcome these odds. Suffice to say that Miss Green received her degree from Franklin Hospital in New Hampshire, the last graduation class consisting of only seven disciplined and dedicated ladies in white.

Boarding at 8 Garfield, which meant: sharing a bedroom with some kitchen privileges in a private residence for three dollars a week, commuting home to the village of Bridgeton via bus on her days off: which meant caring for her younger brothers and

Greenie at 8 Garfield
Starched, Capped and Ready to Go

helping Annie May. Greenie began her long career at Roger Williams. Like any novice, she went from wing to wing, from ward to ward until she found her niche in the pediatric center. Here her special talents and special kind of love dovetailed, giving her the most rewarding and taxing aspects of her self-chosen profession.

I am told that it was not unusual for her to return to the ward after a full day's work: to rock a frightened infant to sleep, to read to a restless child scheduled for surgery or to recheck the dressings on the horrifying burns of a young boy, whose particular case made it into the medical journals. Many a phone call went out from 8 Garfield (her second home for more than thirty-nine years) to calm the fears of anxious parents before Greenie retired for the evening. These giving and gratifying years flew by, and it became obvious to all that she was wearing herself out for the charges left in her care. A kind doctor, who knew her both as a nurse and a patient, stepped in and warned her that if she kept up this pace her skills would soon be of no value to anyone. This logic won the day, and she tearfully left pediatrics and moved to the surgical ward. This, of course, never curtailed her *specializing* on every relatives,' neighbors' or friends' youngsters who found it necessary to *visit* the hospital for surgery.

I often wonder how many patients saw Miss Green hovering protectively over them as they were wheeled into the OR. How many others were relieved to see her small brisk head as they groped out of the fog of anesthesia...then that flash smile and back-to-business look, assuring them that they were A-OK, allowing them to drift back into a more natural sleep. I wonder as well how many more waited to hear the sound of her voice and her quick step as she returned to duty, knowing that they would soon get preferential treatment, a comforting alcohol back rub—fast becoming an anachronism in nursing care—some interesting conversation and an update on their particular case.

She was never too tired to explain to both patient and relative just what was going on, where they stood and what everyone ought to be doing in the meantime. She did not "cotton to" the endless lingering upon a patient's unhappy personal life – she had a few silent woes of her own, and she was, too many times, in more physical pain than those whom she tended. She was there to instill confidence, to offer optimism and to give the best damn nursing care available. For many this seemed to be the best medicine, certainly putting to shame this present day, falsely empathetic drivel that passes for compassion and understanding. Miss Green was – tardily in my estimation – to receive the outstanding Nurse of the Year award of 1969-1970, from Roger Williams Hospital.

In all truthfulness, Greenie was not everyone's cup of tea, nor was everyone hers. Her voice tended to be on the shrill side, a situation she attempted to modulate with varying degrees of success. Her movements were swift, deliberate and accurate. She could inject a syringe of medication or withdraw the needed sample of blood without the patient ever knowing the *operation* had taken place. She had deep and abiding prejudices…not of the color/creed variety but rather for the human characteristics of indolence, irresponsibility, shiftlessness and being uncommitted. Her wrath remained unabated for those who were gifted with many talents and chose neither to make use of them nor to benefit mankind with them. Yet, when they of such odious attributes were ill and in her care, she offered the usual infinite amount of patience, compassion and devotion. When they were on their feet once again, they returned to their deserved graceless state.

As you can imagine, Miss Green did not suffer fools gladly…especially those fools in the medical profession. Many a doctor's ear stung after being upbraided by this mere mite of a being because she believed that he had neglected a patient, leaving him or her in needless discomfort, or that he had failed to pay full attention to the nurses' notes concerning a specific case. She never fudged for an errant doctor who was not where he ought to have been. Older and wiser doctors listened to her pleas for her patients, knowing

Miss Green and
a Portion of her
"Children" off to The
Boston Museum of
Science

Greenie's thoroughness and careful attention to symptoms and the reactions to medical treatment.

But, time changes standards of excellence, and when the "starchiness" of the uniform and of those who inhabited them began to go out-of-style, Miss Green was fast becoming an anachronism herself. Younger doctors and students did not always appreciate Miss Green's demanding dedication and no-nonsense attitude toward the medical profession. Yet, she was known to offer a badly shaken intern *suggestions* concerning a much-needed medical procedure or quietly helped a worthy student who was having a rough spot in her training period. She also realized that the role of head nurse was becoming mostly that of an administrator, feeding a paper lion which devoured too much precious time that could be better spent elsewhere. She stepped down as head nurse during the last few years of her nursing career and gladly returned to the floor to be in direct contact with the needs and wants of the patients. On April 1, 1975, Greenie retired, mostly due to failing health.

When very young my aunt had two wishes or desires, to be an RN, the other to be the mother of twelve. She never got the second wish, but instead loved, cared for, *mentored,* educated, helped support, and nursed back to health twelve times twelve. Some from babyhood through adulthood and others, temporarily, as the need arose. There were suitors; she was an attractive woman, whose energy and curiosity attracted the braver sort. She turned them all down, or they withered away for lack of encouragement.

The retirement years left her free to do other things. On just about any rainy weekend at her home would be found, around her walnut kitchen table, a variety of youngsters playing Monopoly or some newfangled game; or baking a cake for a mother's birthday or for some special holiday.

Egg shells, flour and frosting were scattered all over the place, but there were happy, smiling faces everywhere.

In the evening, around the same table, would be one or two of the older neighborhood children studying…and she was quick to admonish them if their thoughts began to stray. She was forever organizing expeditions to the Boston Museum of Science, Mystic Seaport or to our State Capitol Building. It was an odd assortment, a white haired lady with several non-related looking young girls and boys, with one or two older ones to keep the crew in line. She thought it was her duty and pleasure to bring city children into the country for fresh air, swimming, fishing and cookouts…and to teach them that berries grew on bushes along with the fact that not all animals were domesticated or friendly.

Dare I list her other activities? Every summer she conducted a children's program at the village library, tutored one-on-one for the remedial reading program at the primary school, delivered Meals-on-Wheels throughout the community, tended her sizable vegetable garden and her beloved flower gardens. Her heart was content when she was canning or preserving bushels of pears and peaches to be given away at Christmas time, or knitting little things—a rare treat—for the youngest generation who were climbing onto the family tree. And, there was always the invisible shingle on her door, for those who had eyes to read, "Resident Nurse and Neighborhood Counselor." I best stop here with praise and tribute before you suspend your belief. You might be wondering whether or not the loaves of bread that Miss Green cast upon the waters were ever returned multifold. I judge not. I do know that others have benefited from her casting more than she. She would want it that way anyhow.

My Father's Sled

Today is the anniversary of my father's *crossing over* as I prefer to say, or *Crossing The Bar*, as Alfred Lord Tennyson wrote in his famous poem. Both terms suggesting—Tennyson's less sure than mine—that what we call death is a continuity not an ending, rather a temporary separation (a bar) from the living. My father's passing over had not been easy. "Sorry, there are no miracle drugs to kill the pain from *carcinomatosis*; one can only hope for temporary respites." (Ironically, the fact that he had neither caroused nor smoked in his youth—the church fathers had told him that his body was a temple—and he had paid close attention to physical fitness in the advancing years, only served to prolong the agony.) During these coveted "respites," he talked mostly about his early childhood. Those were the few times that life came back into his eyes.

He chuckled over the fact that when his sister was born, he and his younger brother were relegated to the attic. When it rained, the sounds on the tin roof disturbed them not but rather lulled them to sleep. During the winter months, they found snow dust on the thick quilts that his grandmother had made. The tiny framed home located near a pond not only housed his family but also a progression of widows, widowers, maiden aunts and even a great uncle who had been wounded in the Civil War. They were all a part of his early education.

Ice fishing and snaring small game were not idle winter sports but mean necessity. In the warmer months, gardening, blueberrying and fishing in the many nearby streams added food to the cupboard. In the fall, the gathering of cranberries from an old bog and varied nuts from surrounding woods was insurance that the holidays would be festive. He never failed to mention *Peggy*, who trotted behind or in front of him wherever he went. He enjoyed reliving what we would call hardship today.

Seven months is a long time. In almost every family, the care of the *dying* is left and accepted by one of its members...usually the daughter or the one who lives nearby. My brother, who was in Colorado at the time, flew home as much as he could. Every time he left, he would say, "I don't know how you stand this," and flew away. For some strange reason, the child who has chosen to remain near hearth and home is always the one who cares for and about everything and everybody. This has been true since Biblical times; those who stay appear to be less thought of for it...and that is difficult for the caregivers to accept.

I was never my father's favorite child, being born a girl may have thrilled the family as it continued the one girl per generation tradition, but he would have gladly thrown tradition to the wind if I had been a boy. As they say today, it is a man thing, stemming from those same old Biblical times...an inclination not easy to shake. My brother followed me five years later...much to everyone's joy including mine. As the gods would have it, I was the one to enjoy ice hockey as soon as the pond froze; I was the one with ball and bat in hand scrounging up a team. I can remember, vividly, one soft spring night after an impromptu neighborhood game, my father, shaking his head with a bemused mixture of dismay and admiration, saying to my mother, "Why is *she* the one fleet of foot? Why is *she* the one with the good hand and eye coordination?" In fact, until I was three or four I thought that my real name was *she*. It was always, "What has *she* done now? She has, has *she*? Well, *she* will have a few more chores this week." Not before those seven months had I heard my father call me by my name.

Not that he ignored me as he was always pushing me to do something that he liked to do...such as tennis or studying math and the sciences; all of which were a natural for him...though not for me...so I thought. My father and I argued continuously.

No matter which side of a local, state or federal issue he was for, I was automatically against. We would "word it out" until he used his greater authority to end the conversation. (We would have made a great debating team.) We both stood by our principles and our honor no matter whom we hurt in the process. One such stand off left him silent with me for years. Only when I saw the early pain on his face was that silence broken.

My stubbornness kept me from playing his favorite sport, tennis. I ought to have played and enjoyed this game in my youth. When my daughter came home from college breaks, he urged her to learn how to play...he would pay for the lessons. (He did not give up on an idea easily.) As the fates would have it, daughter needed someone to practice with...I was the chosen one. I became the avid player while she was lukewarm at best. (Perhaps she took it up to please him...they had become great buddies when she was in her teens.) My father was upset to learn that she could not beat me; he immediately had her signed up for a one term course when she returned to school...to no avail, I might add. In the summer months, we played on the high school courts. (We all knew about the *stranger* slowly taking his life from him, though he was not in the critical stages, living at his home, driving his car, etc.)

One afternoon we called him to see if he wanted to watch us play at the school. It did not take him long to get there. He got out of the car in his tennis shorts and carrying three of his treasured racquets...much to our dismay. What could we do? He was determined to play...had been waiting for years to beat me, I suppose. He became her shadow partner returning the balls she might miss. "Two against one is not fair," I said. "What, a dying old man and a young girl...ought to be a piece of cake for you." Before too long the *stranger* who had invaded his body was forgotten while we engaged in battle...as many have said: tennis is not a game but civilized war. I won only a few games as they both were out to get me...no question about it. I knew he was having

Father During World War 11

the time of his life…I also knew how much I had missed in life due to my (and his) stubbornness. It was a wonderful afternoon with much shouting and laughter…a family whole and together. Sometimes I wonder if my daughter had planned all this, or was it a gift from the gods? We both worried about the effects this might have upon him and sent him home to a warm bath and rest. The next day he was so invigorated that he drove up to New Hampshire to see his brothers—his last trip.

The underlying problem between my father and myself had been the fact that we were too much alike and failed to recognize this fact in time. I believe we were given that seven months to ease away the anger and the pain between us. He trusted me, as he always had, to take care of whatever needed to be done. At the nursing home, I was there—as was his younger brother, every day—driving the nurses and doctors up the wall with my demands…reasonable ones to ease his physical pain. When his pain became too much for me to bear, I would escape into the room provided for those who serve and wait. The medical center was near his home; many familiar faces came and went. Over and over, I heard what a good man he was, hardworking and honest to a fault. He never charged enough for his services; they were ashamed to pay the little he asked. Yet, he was able to salt away enough in order that he never would be dependent on his children, community or state. At one time, he had had a well paying position that he had quit the moment the company became unionized. His stubborn stock never knew an intermediary between God and the individual, and there was, definitely, no need for one between boss and worker.

Finally the end came, and I know not why, but was comforted to know that I had been there at the moment of death. His lips had become parched and cracked. I had just finished moistening them with a glycerine swab, and had said, "Now isn't that better?" His eyes were clouded with drugs; he made an attempt to shake his head, yes. The eyes closed and his head slumped forward.

"Thank God," was my immediate response. I had prayed for this release for so long, and now it had come. Instantly, I knew that I really did not want his going. I felt alone and quite defenseless.

I was named, in the will, as executrix of the small estate. This meant more than just *sweeping up the memories*; it also meant combing out all the left behinds. I found the sled hidden, and carefully placed, in back of a pile of odds and ends in the garage. It was so tiny that I thought it was a toy at first. Upon closer inspection, I saw that it was a young child's sled made by hand—the kind that antique seekers dream of finding in a dark corner somewhere. My father's three initials in large block letters were on the underside of the sled in the color that he had painted his cottage a few years back. This was clearly—though a belated one—a statement declaring that, "This is mine!"

Both his father and grandfather had been carpenters. I wondered which one of them had made it for the three or four year old boy. One slat on the top was rough hewn and carelessly nailed to the frame. Both the wooden runners and the frame had been skillfully made. There were two gracefully carved hand holds on the sides so that a child could lug the sled up the hill, placing it in front of him as protection against the icy winds. Hand shaped steel rods were cleverly attached to the runners allowing for more speed. This settled the question; the sled had been made for my grandfather by his father, who had been a skilled craftsman; whereas, his son (my grandfather) had only been a *rough* carpenter. The sled was a legacy from fathers to sons. I can easily visualize my father as a young boy swishing down the hill near his home…the very same hill that my brother and I had used for a winter's playground. I could also imagine my father pulling his younger brothers or sister upon it over snowy hill and dale. Yet, none of them would have dared to use it unless under his tutelage. It had become a rare and precious item to be kept through the years. I had never seen the sled before.

I carefully placed it into the trunk of my car; I brought it home and stored it away for the time being. (This was to be mine!) Today, I remembered and went down to the cellar to study the sled anew. With warm water and soap, I scrubbed the layers of dirt away, debating whether or not to scrape it down for varnishing or for painting. Somewhere from an inner part of me, that I never knew existed before, came a storm of rage, grief, sorrow and despair. The shock of recognizing those sounds as coming from my being left me without breath. Finally, I wept; I wept for all the losses between father and daughter.

My husband found me, exhausted and crying softly, still bent over the sled. Knowing me well, he quietly said, "We will finish this on the weekend. Where are we going to place it...in the foyer?" My voice back to normal said, "The foyer? You mean the front hallway, don't you? Let's call a spade a spade. After all, I am 'She,' my father's daughter.

Gertrude May

It is a quirk of fate that my mother's middle name was the same as that of her mother-in-law, Annie May. Grandmother and her two sisters were known as the Gory Girls, and my mother and her sister were known as the Usher Girls. (Who can hear the name Usher without thinking about Edgar Allan Poe's *The Fall of the House of Usher?*) The Gorys and the Ushers were not related at all except for the fact that both families had ancestors from Wales (one to a greater degree than the other). Nor were they aware of each other, though both families lived in the same village…until of course my father spied Gertrude May. The fact that the families did not know each other in this small community can be explained: Mother's family were Episcopalian and Father's were Baptist. In this little community there were at least seven or eight different Protestant churches as well as three or four Catholic churches…and the parallel lines never met. My father was two years older than my mother; she was twenty years old when they married.

The Gory girls were noted for their proud demeanor and handsome looks; the Usher Girls were noted for their grace and beauty…as you will see in the photographs. One would have thought the Ushers had come from a wealthy family, which was not the case. Their father was the only sibling to have been born in the United States, and their mother was the daughter of Maggie and Michael Kelley, who no doubt came over from Ireland during the potato famine. The Gory girls never inherited their mother's farm in Massachusetts; their widowed mother remarried a much younger man who finagled all that he could from her and then disappeared. Both sets of sisters went to work at sixteen in other people's homes or in the many small mills in the area to support themselves. Still, the Gorys and the Usher Girls (a generation apart) had an aura about them of being ladies—something women strived for no matter what their circumstance in that day and age. Perhaps it was this aura that attracted my father to my mother…sensing or seeing something in common with his own mother when she had been younger.

The relationship between mother and daughter is a complex one and goes through several metamorphoses throughout the various decades…even continuing after the *crossing over* of the mother. In fact it takes many years to think through the strong yet fragile connection between mother and daughter. As far as I can recall the first six or seven years of my life, I adored my mother. Being the only child, I had her full attention…and that of my grandmother and aunts and uncles. Gertrude May had unusually long hair reaching way below her waist. (My hair never would grow that long no matter how much I brushed it.) Mother would sit at the vanity table and let me undo the braids that formed a coronet around her head. Her slightly dark brown hair revealed threads of red when the sunlight danced upon it. It would be wavy from the braiding. I would brush and brush it until the electricity made her hair stand out; I could see the sparks…and feel them too. When I brushed her hair, I would always smell the fragrance of violets. Any hair from the brush was put into an amber colored dish beside the other mysterious feminine jars and tiny bottles. The last time I was with my brother, I asked him if he could remember her when she was young with her long hair. He sadly shook his head to indicate that he did not. I cannot recall when she cut her hair, but I do remember my father's reaction. She had not consulted him regarding this action; he was understandably furious about the lack of consultation and the results of the bobbing of her hair. He sulked for weeks, spoke to no one, finally accepting the deed as a done thing. Looking back, she might have been pregnant with my brother, a fact of which I was unaware. It was summer time, and she would have a lot to do and could not be bothered with the time that it took to maintain her crowning glory. Like my father, I reveled in my mother's beauty…at that stage jealousy had not slithered its way into my heart.

With much hindsight on my part, the cutting of her hair and the birth of my brother were events that began to change our relationship. As I mentioned before, I was not jealous of my brother but was rather curious and intrigued with him…quite proud of him as a matter of fact. Though, there was less time to spend with mother. I had become a part of the neighborhood gang by then and interested in outdoor activities and games inside on rainy days. Too, I was allowed to go to Grandmother's house at will now. My attention was scattered and my world was growing larger. However, I would still go out and cut wildflowers for my mother when she seemed tired or down. Queen Anne's Lace, Black-Eyed Susans and White Daisies filled the house. She carefully made a great deal of fuss over my child-crumpled bouquets.

Grandmother had already begun my education in her fashion; and her daughter, my aunt, introduced me to the world. We went to Boston to museums, suitable plays, book stores and sought out historic spots that were not highly profiled as they are now. We also had lunch and/or tea in a fancy, hotel dining room. I was awe struck by the surroundings and anxious about all the utensils, glasses and dishes arranged on the table. Eventually, I learned the *whyfore* of most of them…though one can never be too secure about this business as different countries, indeed, different regions have their own unique use and placement of silverware and china. I did not know it, but I was growing up and leaving my mother's gentle sphere. I am sure that she was surprised, if not dismayed, that I turned into such a tomboy and sports enthusiast as well as being argumentative, opinionated and forever restless and curious. (Mother always said I was born with a tiny soapbox clutched in my hand, which I continued to carry throughout my life, dragging it out and mounting it at a moment's notice.) I would relate all my adventures to Mother at the supper table or

Sarah Caroline
Usher (l)

Gertrude May
Usher (r)

when she was free to listen to me. She smiled, but I saw
of sadness in her eyes.

Most young children think their mother beautiful…and
the best of circumstances continue to think so forever. However
I soon learned that other people thought my mother fair as well.
Even friends would say, "How pretty your mother is." It made
me proud, but it also grew weary when I realized I was plain as
mud. I wore my hair short with bangs, Buster Brown style until
I was in grammar school. Looking in the mirror, I did not see my
mother's soft blue eyes, her long lush hair, her perfect nose, forehead, mouth, cheeks…all in classic proportion. She had a sweet
and gentle nature and never allowed her anger to control her.
Though my brother looked more like me, he had her nature and
deliberate ways as well as inheriting her musical talents.

Mother's father had remarried. This wife did not allow him
to visit his adult children or his grandchildren, even though, at
one time and quite by mistake, they lived next to my house and
less than a quarter mile from mother's. Once or twice, he would
surreptitiously stop to see my mother for a moment or two, never
sitting but shifting from one foot to the next.

Gertrude May would be so happy that he had stopped by,
and I would scowl at him and think him a miserable excuse of a
man. (Why is it that people whose mothers or fathers leave them,
for whatever reason, are adored by those they leave behind? Is it
that the far away parent is idealized by the youngster beyond any
touch of reality?) I am not sure that I could have been so forgiving
as my mother and her sister. My cousins, much later in life, told
me that their mother, my aunt, adored her father as well…much
to our common disgust.

According to all family stories, the musical ability came from
the Usher family. Pictures of Grandfather show a somewhat ef-
fete but nice looking man with a certain amount of presence. His
aunt and her son had a band that played at the various dances in
the area when jazz was the in thing.

William Usher

And, Great Aunt Hannah was no slouch on the upright piano in her home. Almost everyone had a favorite instrument or sang well. The American Gothic Episcopalian church near Aunt Hannah's home rang out with the musical ability of the Usher family. Mother began to sing early in the church choir and later at the church of choice by my father. Brother carried on the Usher talents but not for public consumption…only for his own pleasure. This too diminished as he became involved in other passions. Mother was disappointed that I had no musical talent; lessons would have been a waste of money. Besides I had no inclination or desire to learn. However, I would sneak into the house, remaining still as a mouse, to listen to her play and sing when she thought no one was around; a stolen, treasured time for me. Still, I did feel sad that I had failed her somehow by not possessing the Usher's musical gene.

In his youth, "Billy" Usher thought he was the cat's pajamas… as we used to say. He was fair of complexion, unlike some Welsh, and his hair tended toward a shade of red, which explains my mother's threads of red…that DNA never lets up! Grandfather considered himself a cut above all the local unpolished and unsophisticated male population…Yankee clouts, Irish clods and the French-Canadian canuks. He was a semi-professional singer on community stages, in churches and at weddings. Nevertheless, he had to work as a commoner for his living. How he met and married the daughter of Michael and Maggie (Hennessey) Kelley is a mystery to all…probably the call of one Celt to another after some stage appearance. This grandmother was a shadow figure in our lifetime. I had seen her once or twice while she was living in Southbridge. She was a large framed woman (like the Gory Girls) with a flawless complexion, Irish blue eyes and that wonderful white, white (not gray) hair of the elderly Hibernians. I never liked her, perhaps by instinct, or more likely, by the fact that she walked out of her home and left three young children to fend for themselves. Grandfather Usher foisted the children upon members of his family, then Grandmother and Grandfather both went about their merry yet separate ways. Mother related her growing up years to me and the aching hurt of being abandoned more or less by both parents. Gertrude May was about five her sister eight and her brother about two. It was forever a saddened cloud that shadowed her heart. She would never abandon a family knowing the damage it would leave behind. I am sure that she did not tell me this so that I would despise her family. Rather, it was an explanation for her silent moodiness that seized her now and then, making her aloof, although she continued the function of running a household, steady as ever.

Of course, I would despise her parents, thinking them little better than slugs in the garden for hurting my mother this way. On the rare occasions of a visit from either one, my father would leave the house without a word spoken, and I would stay and glare at them. Thankfully, my brother was too little to understand but picked up the unfriendly vibrations from my father and me, shying away from them as best he could. My father had the added burden of knowing that his mother's mother had shrugged off her three teenage daughters for a younger man. As you can imagine, family wholeness and loyalty were the prime principles that governed Annie May's family. Family was sacrosanct and came first before anyone's wants or desires. In fact, principles in general were probably held too high in Annie May's family. It was another twist of fate that "Billy Usher" and his *lovely wife* moved into a cottage on the same street where I lived. He was downsizing his lifestyle. Obviously, he did not know it was his granddaughter who lived on top of the hill, although he must have known that Gertrude May lived a quarter of mile down the road. In the winter months, the children used the hill for sledding. When the snow, hardened from the cold, became a slippery glaze of ice, their sleds swished down the hill at top speed. Unable to stop, they swept, once or twice, into Billy's backyard. He was immediately out the door yelling and shouting at them. The boys responded something to this effect, "Cool it, Grampa, we will be more careful next time." I had not encouraged this behavior; however, parents' dislikes pass to their children similar to the process of osmosis in a cell. Besides, they knew he had hurt their grandmother for whom they had a great deal of love and loyalty.

Time went by. One afternoon my mother received a knock on the door. The delivery man handed her the remains of her younger brother in a box postmarked Hawaii. (Her brother, Harold, had joined the service at age fifteen and more or less disappeared. Many years later, she had received a letter from his wife informing Mother that her brother was alive and well, living in Hawaii.) She did not get his wife's note that he had *passed over* before the remains arrived. Our clan immediately gathered around to see what could be done to comfort Gertrude May. Surprisingly a few days later, her father appeared at the door. I was not there so cannot recount the details. At any rate, he handed my mother the deed for a sizable burial lot at Acote's Hill in a nearby community in order that his son be suitably buried…and for use as a family plot for my mother, where there was a baby girl (who had died at birth) resting. (Mother sleeps there now with my father, her brother and the baby sister, Jessie.) Shortly thereafter, Mr. and Mrs. Usher sold their home and moved to another state…never to be heard from again. My parents' resting spot is on the side of a hill overlooking the village; I can see the light rose-colored gravestone as I drive by. I wave to them and sometimes have a few words to say.

Gertrude May liked delicate and lovely things: handkerchiefs (in a day when they were not only used but displayed) with lace on the edges, glassware with fluted edges and a touch of lavender on the rim, crocheted doilies not to put on the backs of furniture but for table tops where vases of flowers could be placed without staining the finish. Sachets (of violet or lavender fragrance) were placed in every drawer of her bureau; everything elegantly arranged. Of course, she enjoyed poetry, music and dressing up for special (and rare) occasions.

Mother liked to be surrounded by people; her door was always open and a welcome always available. People floated in and out at will, driving the rest of us crazy. Father, Brother and I liked our privacy and, at times, our individual solitude. Our door was never locked. On rainy days the gang ended up at our house – nobody else wanted their home messed up – in the spare room upstairs where we played ongoing games of Monopoly, put together complicated puzzles and created stage productions.

Mother and Brother were soft spoken; neither one of them enjoyed arguments (discussions) among family members or strangers; both believing silence was the better response…turning away from wrath. Both she and my brother were deliberate – down right slow in my estimation – in physical actions and reactions. It was agony to shop with her. In twenty minutes, at the most, I could be in and out of a grocery store with all that I needed for a family of five, while Gertrude May puttered around for hours talking to everyone that she met…a social occasion for her. We finally came to a solution about our weekly food shopping. We both started out together: I shopped, went home, put the groceries away, finished a task in progress, reread some material done the night before, had a light lunch, then went down to pick her up, helped put her groceries away and shared a cup of tea with her before returning home. She never really cared about going to New Hampshire as it meant doing the same things that she did at home: cooking, washing and taking care of all of us without the conveniences found in the home…while we frolicked about camping, swimming, hiking and the inevitable hunting for blueberries. (When I became a mother, camping in a tent or living in a hut was no longer an adventure. One became a pioneer woman while others pranced about in the sunshine! One's perspective all depends upon where one is standing.)

Gertrude May married into a family; a family who were: highstrung, argumentative, competitive amongst each other, permanently restless and curious, and quick to anger. They also relished physical activity and reveled in the out-of-doors. They were fiercely loyal to one another, hard workers, did not suffer fools gladly, did not give two hoots about style or fashion preferring something sturdy and lasting...and who forever carried (uneasily) the stigma of having been *poor*. As you can imagine, there were clashes to be had with such oppositions of personalities and character. I say, rather shamefacedly, that I usually sided with my father; my brother with my mother. As time went by, Annie May's son began, belatedly, to accept the fact that I was a girl, but a girl who liked everything that he did, and who would argue with him with fervor. I would also caddy for him just to be on the golf course...and to keep everyone's score. The first time, I padded his card, thinking the higher the number the better chance of his winning. At first he was outraged; as it gradually became an amusing story to tell...he told it often. I have never lived it down along with my disgust with all the people atop Mt. Washington who had arrived there without the hassle of climbing.

We would often times tease my mother about her ways, complaining about her creating her best desserts for her social gatherings or dressing up in a gown for the annual meeting of the Rebeccas. It was unlikely that a housewife in this time period would wear a gown or have any occasion to do so. *Gowns* were not bought at chic shops but rather made on the sewing machine at home.

Gertrude May would agonize for weeks about a pattern and the material to be selected...both from a local department store. No matter, she would emerge from the bedroom looking so lovely that we dared not tease her at all. Though to be honest as her sister-in-law had said, she could make a house dress (remember those?) look like a Dior creation. I disappointed her again by not joining any of the organizations that she favored. In fact both my father and I would laugh at the ceremonies and secret (and harmless) pledges made on initiation night to welcome new members.

(Today, I recognize that all of this elaboration was a need not only for Gertrude May but for humankind. Think about the various organizations that both men and women join to fulfill that need to be part of a special group of people…for ceremony, for rituals, for security, for social acceptance and for form along with pomp and circumstance. Sad to say too many of these *societies* have been downgraded and are mainly used for networking by the ambitious younger crowd.) When Mother left us behind, I found her Rebecca jewelry carefully wrapped in tissue paper and tucked away amongst her other treasures. These were proof of her gradually obtained degrees…none of which I understood. I did not feel she would want me to have them, as I was so mean (read *jealous*) when she was using her time other than for us. A good friend and lifelong neighbor to my mother was pleased that I gave them back to the Rebeccas for future use.

We can, as the wise say, be certain that change will always be. From birth to six or seven, I was my mother's child, seeking her approval and attention, basking in her tender care. From seven or so to fourteen or so, I was my father's shadow trying to keep up with everything he did…even the outside work of gardening and mowing the lawn. (The only curious exception was tennis…some youthful quirk of mine, I am sure.) Mother said little and was teaching my brother piano by that time. Annie May's family and ways were taking over. I was spending more and more time at Grandma's or with my aunt gadding about. At the time, I had not known this was hurting my mother. I was a thorn in her side…but not intentionally. She could not understand my restlessness, my curiosity, my spouting off, my need to be outside, my need to know, my thick-headedness et al. I admit, in hindsight, that I was a stubborn even an impossible child for her to raise. Once in a rare moment of anger, she said, "I hope you have a child just like you." Mother got her wish.

The relationship between mother and daughter is in a constant stage of flux. There are, sometimes, landmarks that we can recall when dramatic changes are occurring; however, most of the time it is a gradual and a diffused metamorphosis. One of the landmarks for me was the beginning of World War II. Father's contribution to the war effort kept him from home weeks on end. I can still feel my father's hands pressing on my shoulders and his eyes looking dead into my eyes to be sure that I was absorbing his serious message. I was given clear and definitive duties to perform while he was away, absent from the hearth. In essence I was to take his place while he was gone: to protect Mother and Brother and to help Grandmother when needed; to keep kindling wood in the wood box in order that Mother could cook; to mow the lawn and take care of the sizable vegetable garden (Brother was assigned the potato bug routine much to my delight); to wash the floors and to help with the always-on-Monday laundry (an all day job); to do the marketing when necessary and so forth and so on.

At first, I thought this meant I would be unable to go to school, but Gertrude May said, laughingly, that I would have plenty of time to do so. I took this responsibility very seriously… and have continued to take responsibility overly serious throughout my life. Both my mother and father knew that there were other resources around besides yours truly: good neighbors, aunts and grandmother as well. A kindly neighbor chopped the kindling wood before I got home from school; another gentleman harrowed the garden while he was doing his own; and my brother not only behaved well (He must have really been read the riot act!) but also helped me as much as he was able to do. I was very proud of myself…almost as proud as being the chosen one to climb Mt. Washington with my father.

My mother kept a straight face – though her eyes gave her away – while I discussed how things were to be done and when. It was great fun for awhile, but I began to realize the amount of hard work and careful organization that it took for my mother to manage the household; I also began to look at her through different eyes and with greater esteem. A war was being waged. When the air raid sounded – just a test – we had to shut off most of the lights and pull the heavy war-time shades (blackout curtains) down. If the warden came, we scrambled under the table…for protection from any would-be flying objects. We were deadly serious about this drill at first, but as time went by we saw it as being funny. Mother, Brother and I would crouch under the table; one of us would giggle, causing all of us to start laughing until the tears rolled down our faces. We took the suggested emergency first-aid program at the local library, I believe on Tuesday nights. Brother was a bit put out that he could not go due to his age and had to stay with Grandmother. We learned pressure points to stop the bleeding in various parts of the body; we rolled bandages and learned how to bandage difficult spots like the ankle or the elbow. We were also taught the art of resuscitation.

It was practiced on a dummy but not done the same way as in modern times. Neither Mother nor I was very good at it; we were told to practice on each other at home. (If one is not in the desperate act of saving a life; it does look rather ridiculous.) Brother would start his famous chuckle as he watched us (He refused to be a victim). We usually all ended up on the floor and laughing. This was a mother that we had not known. It took a war to break down barriers that we never knew existed. The three of us became a solid unit, learning and working together. Mother confided in me, and we solved problems together. I became very protective of her and my only sibling.

One afternoon, she walked a little under a mile to the doctor's office. She had a nasty looking infection around the fleshy tissue between the thumb and first finger, probably a scratch became infected with the harsh soaps used for cleaning. I stayed at home with Brother and a few of the neighborhood gang. Imitating *Tom Sawyer,* I convinced all that we should surprise my mother by cleaning the kitchen. First we did the lunch dishes to be followed by washing and waxing the linoleum floor…no small task. Unlike

Tom, I pitched in so that it would be done properly. Everything was neat and sparkling as she liked to have her kitchen. We sat around waiting and waiting for her to come home. Grandmother appeared to see whether or not Mother was back. She sent my friends and me off down the street pell mell to see where my mother was. We found her seated on a low wall about a quarter of a mile from the house; her hand was bandaged up to her wrist; she was as white as the proverbial sheet.

Mother explained that the doctor had cleaned out the infection with a scalpel without applying any local anesthesia; she had nearly fainted twice in the process. (I knew that she had been crying as well.) I was eager to rush down to the office and kick the doctor in the shins. Mother decided it was best to get her home first. We propped her up and surrounded her…more or less moving her along as we went. When we finally arrived at home, Grandmother and Brother were as furious as we. Both of them were ready to assault the doctor with us. Mother's calm reasoning won the day, saying that she needed us with her. We put her to bed, having given her three aspirin, and tiptoed around the house while she slept. She also had made us promise not to say anything to Father when he came home…though no family member ever made use of that doctor's service from thereafter. (She had noticed the sparkling kitchen and thanked everyone when she awakened.)

Gertrude May never had time to be a child growing up; I believe she had some childhood while we were in the war-time situation. I had just purchased a used bike with money from a paper route—as soon as the coveted bike was obtained, I sold the route. Of course, I knew how to ride and Brother was soon doing the same, although his short legs prevented him from ever sitting on the seat. We insisted that Mother learn as well…she would be able to go to the store, to visit friends or ride up to the pond, etc. She tried. Brother and I would hold each side of the bike and guide and support her while she breezed along; however, as soon as she thought we were not holding her up, down she would go.

We finally gave up, but we had a great deal of fun while she tried. She even went swimming with us, saying an adult ought to be with us—this was news to Brother and I as we had been swimming without one for a few years. We were amazed that she could swim...rather well at that. We had one problem though, Inky our dog. Actually he was supposed to be my brother's, but he had attached himself to me for walks and other activities and to Mother for food and loving care. I was not the only protector of my mother. Inky was the dark guardian of his mistress. He always went swimming with us and would sleep on the beach while we swam—not really caring for the water per se. This was not the case when my mother joined us and went out into deep water. Inky would go wild with fear and concern, jumping into the water, paddling to reach her and then circling around her and barking with terror until she went ashore. (Apparently, he did not care what happened to my brother or me.) Inky would sit on the seat of our square ended rowboat and allowed us to row him around like a prince. Mother decided not to go boating with us, not knowing what Inky would do in this case. We had been enjoying all these out-of-door things with Father; now it was her turn to have some fun with us. Just when Mother was acting like me, I began to take notice that I was indeed a girl entering high school. How I dressed (like everyone else, of course, saddle shoes, long skirts and fluffy sweaters) along with the arrangement of my hair became prime concerns.

This is the age that a daughter needs a mother to confide in, to seek wisdom from and to dry the inevitable tears. It is also the time that the youngsters are yearning for independence and recognition by their peers—a difficult and trying time for all concerned. Mother and I did not engage in long drawn out bathos about all the changes taking place, but she was always available and seemed to know when I needed some straight talk or some *Tea and Sympathy*. Thus, the tea ritual developed between us and lasted through the rest of her life.

If my hair would not behave, if I could not get started on a written school assignment, if I had not been accepted by the in-crowd, if my feelings had been hurt in a million little ways, or if I were in a rage about some political affair; she would go to the cupboard and get the teapot out along with two cups. She boiled water on the stove—like the Japanese it had to be *boiling* water—then steeped the tea an exact amount of time—no more and no less—before we sat down at the kitchen table. She talked in her calm voice as we sipped the tea *sans* sugar or milk. Resolutions were not always forthcoming. But, I felt comforted; my ruffled feathers had been soothed; I could face the situation in a more reasonable manner. Of course, as we both grew older the *ifs* became a tad more serious and consequential...still I always felt reinforced, even restored, after Mother's tea time. The Irish, the British, as well as the Japanese have known the use of this ritual for a long time. (Japanese the longest.) I have her rose flowered teapot and the matching cups on a tray in my dining room—a set the children had given her one Christmas. There were times that I played Mother's role for others and followed the same ritual... perhaps not always with the same results. What I would give to share a cup of tea and a great deal of sympathy—not to mention love—with my ever-faithful and lovely mother.

Gertrude May's loveliness as well as her sister's was a difficult problem for their growing daughters. Aunt Sarah had two daughters and my mother just me. None of us favored either mother to any great degree but took generous doses of the fathers' side of the individual family...though my eldest cousin was quite pretty. Cousins spent two weeks of each summer with one another's family.

It was something I looked forward to with great enthusiasm, until my year older cousin became aware of the boy/girl thing and became far prettier and more feminine than myself. For me the neighborhood gang were all *buddies*...no more no less. Soon she tired of games, boating, swimming and the like—and just hung

around in a frock with all the male members of the gang tongue-
tied and at her feet—much to my disgust. I knew the reaction
to beauty not just of men, but of women, having watched both
mother and aunt receiving the admiring or the envious glances,
the speedier or slower service, and from the males more attention, care and helpfulness...let me carry that package to the car,
too heavy for you...let me get a nicer box for you...could I help
you *et cetera, et cetera, et cetera.*

Now my cousin was getting similar reactions; I wanted some
of that attention as well. In high school I was awkward, shy and
still a tomboy at heart...and in appearance, I put all my efforts
into my studies...at least I would be smart. There was no prom
date for me much to Mother's dismay.

She kept her thoughts to herself. In desperation I decided to
get a permanent, believing the magazine advertisements that one
would turn into the current darling of the screen if only one's hair
was styled by so and so. Mother tried to warn me not to expect too
much. It was an operation that brought tears to my eyes, all that
clipping, tugging and pulling, curling and finally plugged into a
machine that looked like an electric shock treatment mechanism.
Hours of torture and foul smelling lotions dripping down onto a
cape of plastic. Needless to say, I did not resemble any movie
star...my mother...or even me. I saw the tightly–very–clustered
ringlets around my too full Irish face...one of the few features
derived from Gertrude May's genes.

I felt like a shorn sheep must feel losing his/her winter's coat
in the spring. I ran with tears on my face all the way home. Mother reached for the teapot. I was all for shaving my hair–what
was left of it–completely off and starting over, but she patiently
brushed my hair as much as I allowed, had me wash it every other
night while she gradually snipped the ugly dark wool from my
head. We talked about beauty being only skin deep–easy for her
to say–of handsome is as handsome does. Much later, I knew
there was some wisdom in these old sayings: Part of the Usher

girls' charm was their good manners as well as their demeanor and pleasant ways. "Beauty is in the eye of the beholder," she told me. Small comfort, I spent too much of my life trying to look like my mother until I realized it was hopeless. Many family members looked back at me from the mirror: Grandmother's eyes and cheekbones, Greenie's forehead, Mother's lips and chin, and my father was seen very clearly in the over all effect. The nicest compliment that I ever received was delivered by an old friend of my mother's when she said, "As you grow older, you look more like your mother." I am not sure this is true, but we all see through different eyes. Perhaps she saw something: the way I laugh, the way my eyebrows grow, a certain mannerism, or a smile of greeting reminding her of my mother. True, I have *mellowed out* some, have learned to bite my tongue and to guard my snappy replies, have slowed down a bit, have learned that kindness is always welcomed and that it is not wise to take someone's dignity away from them – to do so, you have earned an enemy for life – as the Japanese wisely have known all along.

Gertrude May was born lovely with goodness evenly distributed. I had to learn how to be more pleasing not only from Mother but from hard experience as well. This was similar to her faith in God; there never was any doubt in her mind. She sometimes changed her church association when she was disappointed in the minister or priest, or the congregation; however, it was always clear in her mind what God expected of her. Mother was not showy about this but quietly lived her beliefs by word and deed. Her daughter's (my) constant questioning about faith and the Bible upset my mother badly. The Sunday school teachers were alarmed at my questions that they could not answer with what I considered logical explanations. Faith is not an intellectual puzzle to solve, but for some it is a long and treacherous journey before unquestionable faith graces their soul. It took me a good amount of time. It may have helped that I had a fine example to follow, and as children Brother and I spent many hours on Sundays in church, first Sunday School, later up to the service and back in the evening for Christian Fellowship. During the week nights, Bible Study and many social events for youngsters and the elderly saw members of our family there. It did not do us any harm. Returning to Mother and Aunt Sarah, they were both love-ly until the day they left us behind. With both sisters, the good-ness continued to shine through. I found a picture of my mother, probably in her late teens, while going through her things. It rests beside my night-table next to the bed. She looks straight into my eyes with a shadow of a smile every night. Mother is still calming and comforting me with her warmth and beauty.

As we grow older and have the past to revisit, we often find that things were not always what we thought they were when they were occurring. For instance, my father appeared to me as decisive, strong, courageous with all the manly characteristics once admired in the male. This was true, but it was Mother who had made the difficult family choices and decisions, and it was she who cemented the family together. It amazed me that when they traveled my father was shy and unsure of himself —while out of his sphere so to speak. It was Mother who made the travel arrangements and reservations and dealt with the public at large. She was also the one who signed for me, allowing me to try my wings at eighteen in faraway places…and saw to it that my broth-er went to the school and into the profession that he wanted.

It was I, again, who gave her a bitter pill to swallow when I had my fragile wings broken. Not entirely my fault or my intention to do so. We can skip the boring—for others—details. I turned to home for guidance, for comfort, for courage, for restoration and faithful love. It was hardest on my mother as she felt some guilt for letting me go on my own so young. I had disappointed her once again, but she found the strength along with Grandmother and Greenie to patch me up and get me growing and filled with confidence once again. There was a happy ending to this story.

Mother and Father in Their Golden Years

However, I knew how much it had taxed my mother's strength. (Children rarely know, until they are adults with adult children of their own, how much pain children of all ages can bring to their parents, not meaning to do so.) The remaining years that we had together, I did whatever I could to erase my debt to her.

We shared so many good times together as she did with Brother in the later years. Mother was never of robust health and survived too many operations. Toward the latter part of her life, she grew very tired and had reason to be so. The last operation left her with some paralysis from a stroke suffered in the OR...and not recognized by doctors or staff members, until it was too late. (Would that she could have had Greenie by her side as the nurse.) She lived for nine months just enjoying her family and friends around her. One night my father called asking me to mother-sit for him while he played tennis at the indoor court. Down I went to chat, to share a cup of tea and to put her to bed. She managed to get her own clothes off and left them in a neat little circle on the bathroom floor and slipped into her nightgown, She got into bed, and I tucked her in and ship-shaped the sheets and blanket as Greenie had taught me. Mother was watching me with those blue eyes and smiling; we both burst out laughing, together. Our individual thoughts leaped from one mind to the other in mega-seconds...and it was the same thought! Here was the complete role reversal. How many times had she performed this function for me when I was young or suffering with some childhood illness. Now I was doing this comforting and loving gesture for her. We were completely in tune with one another at long last.

The following night she *crossed over* quietly in her sleep. My father called to tell me around three in the morning. I was told that I said, "It is not so," and went back to bed and slept. I just could not accept the fact and froze it out of my mind. It took a long time, a decade or so, not to rush for the phone to call her and tell her some small disaster or good news about the children or whatever. We had grown so close during the latter part of her life. I can recall stopping on the way home from the dentist, rushing into her house like a child and mocking the radio ad saying, "Look, Mom...no cavities!" She told that to everyone; because the story has come back to me many times. There were few days that we did not see each other at least once, usually twice. Strangely, each year I grow closer to her than while she was with us. I feel her presence everywhere and have kept a few things scattered around the house, though they are not needed for remembrance. It is actually no longer remembrances but rather some way of being with her. I cannot explain it. She has not gone; she still remains with us to keep me from harm's way.

Cleaning out my desk one evening, I felt her close by when I found a poem she had written to me, thanking me for the lovely roses–I was forty-seven when it was written–we had graduated from the wildflower days. I thought her thoughts within the poem revealed so much about her. The lines are still heavenly music to me knowing that, somehow or other, I had given her love and joy.

The roses you brought the other day
Brought back memories of old.
When you were small a tiny tot
playing in a field of gold of
Buttercups and daisies, a child's
delight all told.

So many times you came inside
with tiny hands filled with
all that they could hold.
A shy grin of love and joy
"I picked 'em,' Mama for you."

And as you left the other day
when you went through the door,
I saw again the same shy smile
as was in days of yore.

Afterthoughts

It is my observation that people—with all the myriad means of communication—seem to be lonely. There are many reasons for this from my point of view. The unbelievable state of the individual in our society who appears to think that he or she is the most important person in the world. There is less sense of a cohesiveness amongst family members. (I can recall when cousins were considered intimate members of any family, and acted that way as well.) All too many members of our society think that the state or federal government should be responsible for the care of their elderly parents along with the care of the children that they themselves bear. Family members spend little time with each other. Busy Moms and Dads are no longer the teachers of skills nor do they instill a sense of moral obligation to the family, to the community and to the country. So many youngsters think that history begins the day they were born, as do most of their teachers. Grandmothers and Grandfathers no longer hand down tales of ancestors or a history of the past that they know so well. Material things far outweigh time spent together as a family. Our society has turned into a self-centered and callous place in which to live. Is this what we really want?

JGK

About the Author

The author is a native of (and lives in) Rhode Island. She served three years in the Women's Army Corps during the Korean War. She is a charter member of Women in the Service for the American Memorial Foundation in D.C. While in Tokyo, she attended Sophia University and is also a graduate of Rhode Island College and the University of Rhode Island. She has served her community as President of The Burrillville Historical and Preservation Society, Director of the Burrillville Historic Districts Commission, Board Member of the Pascoag Public Library and a Board Member of the League of Rhode Island Historical Societies from which she received the John Nicholas Brown award for exceptional contributions to the preservation of Rhode Island Heritage.

www.ingramcontent.com/pod-product-compliance
Lightning Source LLC
Chambersburg PA
CBHW020338290526
45785CB00005B/2080